AVOIDANT PERSONALITY DISORDER

Understanding, Managing, and Overcoming

WELLINGTON DOUGLAS

CONTENTS

CHAPTER 1

Identifying Avoidance Personality Disorder

Avoidance Personality Disorder: Definition

Avoidant personality disorder is a mental illness defined by a pervasive pattern of social inhibition, feelings of inadequacy, and hypersensitivity to unfavorable judgment. People with AvPD frequently have a severe fear of being rejected, criticized, or disapproved, which makes them avoid social situations and interactions where they might be judged.

The following are key traits of avoidance personality disorder:

1. Avoidance of Social Situations: People with AvPD frequently shy away from social situations, making new friends, and having to communicate with others.

2. Low Self-Esteem: They frequently have a negative self-perception and think they are unworthy or unlikable by nature.

3. dread of Rejection: They struggle to start or keep relationships because they have a crippling dread of being laughed at or rejected.

4. Limited Interpersonal Relationships: People with AvPD frequently isolate themselves and may have very few intimate relationships, if any at all.

5. Extreme Self-Consciousness: They experience feelings of embarrassment and humiliation because they are extremely self-conscious, especially in social circumstances.

6. Dependence on a Small Number of Trusted People: They might look to a select number of dependable people for assistance and company.

A person with avoidance personality disorder may have distress and functioning impairment in a variety of contexts, including job, school, and interpersonal interactions. People with AvPD may benefit from treatment, which may include psychotherapy and occasionally medication, to better control their symptoms and enhance their social and emotional well-being.

The Effect on Everyday Life

For those who have it, the effects of avoidant personality disorder (AvPD) on day-to-day living can be severe and difficult. AvPD can have the following effects on daily life:

1. Limited Social Interaction: Individuals with AvPD frequently shy away from social interactions, which might result in loneliness. They might turn down social invites, pass up networking opportunities, and have fewer close relationships.

2. Difficulty at Work or School: AvPD can make it difficult for a person to perform successfully at work or in a

classroom setting. It may be difficult to participate in group projects, work collaboratively with coworkers, or ask for assistance when you need it due to a fear of criticism and rejection.

3. Relationship Impact: For people with AvPD, developing and sustaining close relationships can be quite challenging. Their inability to trust others, express themselves, or open up emotionally can make friendships and love affairs difficult.

4. poor Self-Esteem: Self-doubt and poor self-esteem might result from a persistent dread of being evaluated or rejected. People who have AvPD may experience self-worth issues and have a negative opinion of themselves.

5. Avoidance of Opportunities: Avoidance tendencies can result in the loss of chances for new experiences, professional development, and personal growth. Because they are afraid of failing or being rejected, people with AvPD may not pursue their ambitions.

Living with AVPD can result in substantial mental suffering, such as anxiety, despair, and a feeling of loneliness. Chronic stress and emotional weariness might result from constantly expecting negative evaluations.

7. Physical Symptoms: The tension and stress brought on by AvPD can cause physical symptoms like headaches, tense muscles, and digestive issues.

8. Effect on Health: Avoidance tactics may also include going to the doctor when necessary. People with AvPD may put off or forego getting medical care because they feel awkward around others.

While avoidant personality disorder can have a significant negative influence on daily living, there is still hope for recovery. With the proper care, such as counseling and assistance from mental health specialists, people with AvPD can acquire coping mechanisms and form healthy social interaction patterns, which will enhance their quality of life.

The Unspoken Battles

Even though avoidant personality disorder (AvPD) sufferers frequently go unnoticed by others, these problems can be emotionally and mentally upsetting. These covert conflicts include:

1. Extreme Self-Criticism: People with AvPD tend to be overly critical of their own words and actions. They frequently engage in a critical internal conversation that feeds their sense of inadequacy.

2. Fear of Vulnerability: People with AvPD may look reserved or distant, yet they may be quite sensitive and afraid of showing their vulnerabilities. They go to tremendous measures to keep their fears and insecurities hidden.

3. Social Isolation: Strong social isolation might result from a desire to avoid social circumstances and

interactions. Feelings of loneliness and depression, which might not be immediately obvious to others, might be made worse by this isolation.

4. Overanalyzing Social events: AvPD patients frequently repeat social events in their heads, examining each nuance for clues of approval or rejection. It can be mentally draining to dwell on things.

5. Limited Possibilities for Growth: AvPD can prevent people from taking chances or pursuing possibilities, which can impede their personal and professional development. They could pass up opportunities for growth and advancement because they are afraid of failing.

6. Problems with Intimacy: Establishing and sustaining personal relationships can be particularly difficult. AvPD can erect a wall between people's emotional intimacy, making it challenging for people to be vulnerable and establish meaningful connections.

7. Impaired Self-Expression: These people frequently find it difficult to express themselves honestly. They may repress their feelings and ideas out of concern that being who they truly are will cause them to be rejected.

8. Prolonged Stress and Anxiety: Prolonged stress and anxiety might result from a persistent dread of criticism and rejection. Although others might not see this underlying anxiety, it can be extremely demanding.

9. Effect on Self-Esteem: Over time, AvPD can lower self-esteem as sufferers internalize criticism and avoid circumstances that make them question their value.

It's essential to comprehend these unspoken hardships to help and empathize with those who have AvPD. They may not be able to see the problem, but it still has a substantial influence on their everyday lives and emotional health, so they could use some expert assistance as well as a supportive social network.

CHAPTER 2

The Causes and Origins of Avoidance

Psychiatric variables

Avoidant Personality Disorder (AvPD) develops and manifests as a result of many psychological causes. These elements may have a role in the disorder's distinctive traits and difficulties. Here are a few crucial psychological variables:

1. Low Self-Esteem: People with AvPD frequently have deep-seated low self-esteem. They might have unfavorable opinions of themselves and think they're essentially bad people. Their avoidance habits may be influenced by these unfavorable self-perceptions.

2. Early Childhood Experiences: AvPD can develop as a result of adverse childhood experiences such as emotional neglect, rejection, or bullying. A person's underlying views about themselves and others may be

influenced by these events, which can result in social anxiety and a fear of rejection.

3. Negative fundamental views: People with AvPD tend to have negative fundamental views about both themselves and other people. These notions encompass fears of being rejected, severe criticism of oneself, and the notion that others are critiquing or judging. These ideas affect how people see and react to social circumstances.

4. Hypersensitivity to Criticism: People with AvPD may have a high threshold for actual or perceived criticism. They may find even minor feedback or constructive criticism to be quite upsetting, which makes them avoid social situations even more.

5. Cognitive Biases: Cognitive biases might contribute to the anxiety and avoidance behaviors seen in AvPD, such as selective attention to negative social cues and

overestimating the chance of unfavorable outcomes in social interactions.

6. Avoidance as a Coping Strategy: Avoidance strategies are developed as a coping strategy to shield oneself from the prospect of perceived rejection or humiliation. These avoidance tactics develop into habits over time.

7. Fear of Vulnerability: Those who have AvPD frequently worry about showing emotional vulnerability in social settings. They could be reluctant to be vulnerable with others because they think that doing so will make them feel rejected.

Both those who have AvPD and mental health professionals striving to offer support and therapy must comprehend these psychological variables. People can confront and change these unhelpful ideas through psychotherapy, especially cognitive-behavioral therapy (CBT), and find better ways to cope with their symptoms.

Childhood Recollections

Childhood events can have a significant impact on how avoidant personality disorder (AvPD) develops. Even though not all people with AvPD have had traumatic experiences as children, specific kinds of early traumas are frequently linked to the illness. The following childhood events may have influenced the emergence of AvPD:

1. Rejection and Neglect: Childhood experiences of emotional abandonment, neglect, or rejection can leave long-lasting emotional scars. Children who experience rejection or unlove may grow to fear rejection and think they are intrinsically unlikable.

Bullying or Peer Rejection 2. Social Anxiety and a Fear of Social Interactions can be brought on by bullying or persistent peer rejection during childhood. These unpleasant encounters may serve to confirm the notion that people are unfair and unreliable.

3. Controlling or overly protective parenting might impede a child's capacity to gain independence and social skills. Such conditions can make it difficult for kids to feel independent and confident in social settings.

4. Critical Parental Figures: Overly critical or perfectionistic parents or caregivers may be a factor in a child's poor self-esteem. Persistent feelings of inadequacy might be brought on by unrelenting criticism and unattainable expectations.

5. Social Trauma: Negative social experiences, such as being embarrassed or humiliated in front of others, can leave lasting emotional scars. A significant aversion to social situations and interactions may result from these experiences.

6. Modeling Avoidant Behavior: Parents or other key caregivers frequently influence their children's behavior. A youngster may pick up similar avoidance techniques if

a caregiver engages in avoidant behaviors or suffers from social anxiety.

7. The absence of wholesome social role models Lack of good social role models during childhood might restrict a child's exposure to pleasant social interactions and impede social skill development.

It's crucial to remember that, even while these early experiences may have influenced the formation of AvPD, they do not ensure the illness will show up in adulthood. It is complicated how temperament, environmental variables, and genetic predispositions interact. However, knowing these potential risk factors might assist mental health providers in giving persons with AvPD specialized care and interventions. Therapy and counseling can help resolve the effects of early experiences and create more wholesome social interaction habits.

Environmental and genetic influences

Genetic and environmental variables work together to impact the emergence of Avoidant Personality Disorder (AvPD). While genetics may predispose someone to the illness, environmental events have a significant impact on whether or not it appears. These factors interact in intricate ways. An overview of the genetic and environmental factors that affect AvPD is given below:

genetic factors:

1. Family History: People who have an AvPD or other anxiety-related disorder in their family may be more genetically predisposed to having AvPD. Personality traits, temperament, and susceptibility to anxiety can all be influenced by genetic factors.

2. Temperamental Factors: Some people may have temperamental characteristics from birth that make them more prone to worry and avoidance behaviors. For instance, high trait shyness or behavioral inhibition

levels throughout childhood may run in the family and aid in the emergence of AvPD.

3. Neurobiological Factors: According to research, the amygdala and the serotonin system, among other brain regions and neurotransmitter systems, may play a role in anxiety disorders, including AVPD. An individual's chance of having AvPD may be influenced by genetic differences associated with these systems.

Environmental factors

As was already established, negative early events including emotional neglect, rejection, or bullying can have an impact on the development of AvPD. An individual's self-esteem, worldview, and coping mechanisms are shaped by these events.

2. Parental Attachment: The degree of a child's attachment to their primary caregiver(s) can have an impact on how AvPD develops. Later in life, it may be

challenging to build trusting connections as a result of insecure or chaotic attachment patterns.

3. Social learning: Children pick up new skills by seeing and copying the actions of others around them. They may develop comparable avoidance behaviors if they are raised in an atmosphere where social anxiety or avoidance is encouraged or imitated.

4. Traumatic situations: Particular traumatic experiences or situations, such as being severely rejected by others or being humiliated in public, can cause or aggravate the symptoms of AVPD. Trauma can influence a person's social interaction-related beliefs and phobias.

5. Cultural and sociological factors: Cultural and societal norms might have an impact on how AvPD is expressed and understood. Societies that place a strong emphasis on individualism or excellence may help those who are sensitive to AvPD develop.

It's crucial to remember that while environmental and genetic risk factors can increase the likelihood that someone will develop AvPD, not everyone who carries these risk factors will. Individual experiences differ greatly due to the intricate interaction between heredity and environment. Regardless of the underlying causes, individuals with AvPD can control their symptoms and improve their quality of life with early intervention and proper treatment, such as psychotherapy.

CHAPTER 3

Understanding the Symptoms and Signs

Patterns of Common Behaviour

People who have an avoidant personality disorder (AvPD) frequently display typical behavioral patterns of the illness. These patterns represent their efforts to manage the underlying concerns and fears they have about social engagement and possible rejection. Here are some typical AvPD-related behavioral patterns:

1. Avoidance of Social Situations: The strongest and most enduring pattern is an intense aversion to social interactions and circumstances. To reduce the likelihood of social contacts, people with AvPD may turn down invitations to social gatherings, avoid making new friends, and even postpone simple tasks like going to the shop.

2. Small and Limited Social Circle: They often have a small and limited social circle that consists of their immediate family and a select few reliable pals. It can be difficult to establish and sustain relationships outside of this group.

3. People with AvPD are extremely sensitive to criticism and are afraid of being criticized or ridiculed by others. They frequently are unable to express themselves honestly or participate in discussions or arguments because of this anxiety.

4. Reluctance to Take Chances: AvPD makes people less willing to attempt new things or take chances, particularly in social or professional settings. For fear of failing or receiving bad feedback, they can decide not to pursue opportunities.

5. Self-Isolation: AvPD frequently results in isolation. People who have the disorder may spend a lot of time

by themselves, avoid social situations, and frequently choose solitary pastimes.

6. Perfection: Some AvPD sufferers may exhibit perfectionistic traits to fend off criticism or rejection. They could have unattainable standards for themselves, which might cause stress and inaction.

7. Relationship Initiation Difficulties: Beginning new relationships, whether platonic or romantic, can be difficult. They could find it difficult to strike up discussions or move first in social situations.

8. Self-Criticism: People with AvPD frequently have harsh opinions of themselves and a poor self-image. People could constantly evaluate themselves, concentrating on perceived flaws and deficiencies.

9. Overanalyzing Social Interactions: People with AVPD frequently overthink and ruminate after engaging in social interactions. They mentally repeat discussions,

searching every nuance for indications of rejection or criticism.

10. Physical Symptoms: Social anxiety can cause symptoms like perspiration, shaking, an accelerated heartbeat, and gastrointestinal distress.

It's critical to remember that people with AvPD employ these behavioral patterns as coping methods to control their anxiety and fear of social situations. Therapy and support can help people with AvPD develop more adaptable ways of managing their symptoms and enhancing their social relevance even though these patterns can be constrictive and distressing.

Cognitive and Emotional Signs

People who have an avoidant personality disorder (AvPD) frequently display a variety of emotional and cognitive symptoms that mirror their underlying concerns, fears, and avoidance tendencies. The following examples of symptoms that are typical of the emotional and cognitive experiences of those with AvPD include:

Mood Indices:

1. Anxiety: AvPD is characterized by persistent and severe anxiety. People with the illness frequently exhibit increased anxiety before social events because they worry about being rejected or criticized.

2. dread of Rejection: The main emotional symptom of AvPD is a pervasive, crippling dread of rejection. To escape possible rejection, this anxiety may cause one to shun social situations.

3. Low Self-Esteem: People with AvPD frequently have low self-esteem and a negative view of themselves. They may shun social events out of a belief that they are intrinsically inadequate or unlikable.

4. Depression: People with AvPD may experience depression due to ongoing social isolation and feelings

of inadequacy. It can be emotionally distressing to feel alone and hopeless.

5. People with AvPD are frequently highly sensitive and may retaliate fiercely to perceived slights or criticism. Even seemingly innocuous remarks might elicit strong emotional responses.

6. Shame and Embarrassment: In social circumstances, feelings of shame and embarrassment are frequent emotional reactions. People with AvPD could feel humiliated by their avoidance tendencies and lack of social skills.

Cognitive Symptoms

1. Cognitive Distortions: People with AvPD typically engage in cognitive distortions such as overgeneralization (applying unpleasant experiences to all future social interactions), mind reading (assuming others are adversely assessing them), and catastrophic thinking (expecting the worst outcome).

2. Rumination: People with AvPD frequently engage in rumination after social interactions, repeating conversations and situations in their heads and looking for indications of rejection or criticism.

3. Avoidant thinking: Cognitive tendencies that include the thinking "I'll be rejected," "I'm not good enough," or "People will think I'm weird" are frequent. These ideas help people stay out of social situations.

4. Safety Behaviors: People with AvPD may use safety behaviors to lessen anxiety in social situations, such as practicing talks beforehand. These actions represent an effort to control their fears cognitively.

5. Internal self-talk that is unfavorable is common in AvPD. People could constantly berate themselves and use their thoughts to promote their poor perceptions of themselves.

6. They frequently believe others to be critical and judgmental despite the lack of supporting facts. Their

avoidance of social relationships may be influenced by this impression.

These avoidance behaviors and social withdrawal that are frequently linked to AvPD are influenced by these interwoven emotional and cognitive indicators of the condition. People with AvPD who are in psychotherapy, particularly cognitive-behavioral therapy (CBT), can learn to recognize and fight these harmful thought patterns and create better-coping mechanisms.

Reflection and evaluation of oneself

Self-reflection and assessment are vital activities for improving oneself and growing personally. They enable people to understand their thoughts, feelings, behaviors, and decisions in life. Following are some guidelines and techniques for conducting a good self-evaluation:

1. Find Quiet Time: Allocate specific, unbroken time for introspection. Find a place that is peaceful and

`

comfortable so you can concentrate without being distracted.

2. Journaling: Write your ideas, emotions, and experiences down in a journal. You can identify patterns in your thinking and behavior as well as your emotions by writing.

3. Ask the Right Questions: Pose open-ended queries to yourself that invite introspection. For instance, "What are my long-term goals?" or "What are my strengths and weaknesses?"

4. Review Prior Experiences: Think back on your prior experiences, both good and bad. Think about the lessons you've taken away from them and how they've influenced your ideas and ideals.

5. Specify both short- and long-term goals for your personal development. Self-improvement goals give direction and motivation.

6. Utilize self-assessment instruments or questionnaires according to your areas of interest or concern. These may offer organized insights into your character, principles, and interests.

7. Feedback from Others: Consult with dependable friends, family members, or mentors for their opinions. Others may provide insightful viewpoints on your advantages and weaknesses.

8. Values and Priorities: Identify your values and guiding principles. Your judgments and behaviors might be influenced by understanding what is genuinely important to you.

9. To become more conscious of your thoughts and emotions in the present moment, practice mindfulness and meditation. You can monitor your inner experiences with mindfulness and without passing judgment.

10. Identify Triggers: Recognize persons or circumstances that set off unfavorable feelings or

actions. You may create management solutions for your triggers by understanding them.

11.appreciate Your Successes: Regardless of how tiny they may seem, acknowledge and appreciate your successes. Your motivation and self-esteem can both be increased through positive reinforcement.

12. Seek Professional Assistance: If you're battling complicated challenges or mental health issues, you might want to speak with a therapist or counselor. They can offer direction and support while you go through the process of self-evaluation and personal development.

13. Make self-reflection and appraisal a regular practice, such as once a month or once every three months. You can monitor your progress and revise your goals as necessary by checking in frequently.

14. Accept Imperfection: Recognize that self-reflection may point out areas where you lack or err. Accept

imperfections as a chance for development and education.

15. Create action plans with clear stages and deadlines once you've determined which areas need improvement. To grow personally, one must take action.

Keep in mind that self-analysis and evaluation are ongoing processes. You'll be better able to make wise decisions, establish worthwhile goals, and live a more fulfilling life as you develop an understanding of who you are and what your life is all about.

CHAPTER 4

Choosing a Treatment Option

Therapy Techniques

Treatment for Avoidant Personality Disorder (AvPD) must include therapy. People with AvPD may benefit from a variety of treatment modalities to help them control their symptoms, boost their self-esteem, and create stronger social relationships. The following therapeutic modalities are frequently employed to treat AvPD:

1. Cognitive-Behavioral Therapy (CBT): CBT is frequently regarded as the main treatment strategy for AvPD. It focuses on recognizing and disproving unfavorable mental attitudes and assumptions that support avoidance behaviors and social anxiety. Through CBT, people can learn to change the way they think, feel less anxious, and act in more adaptive ways.

2. Exposure Therapy: In a safe and encouraging setting, exposure therapy gradually exposes patients to social situations they are afraid of. This exposure enables people to face their concerns, lessen their avoidance, and develop their social skills.

3. Group Therapy: Group therapy offers people with AvPD a secure and encouraging environment in which to develop relationships, practice social skills, and get peer feedback. Reducing social isolation and boosting social confidence are two benefits of group therapy.

4. Schema Therapy: AvPD is treated using a longer-term therapeutic technique called schema therapy that focuses on identifying and changing deeply rooted negative schemas or basic beliefs. It addresses problems with interpersonal connections, self-worth, and self-esteem.

5. Mindfulness-Based Therapy: Mindfulness-based therapies, such as Mindfulness-Based Stress Reduction

(MBSR) and Mindfulness-Based Cognitive Therapy (MBCT), can assist people with AvPD in managing their anxiety, reducing rumination, and gaining a better sense of themselves and their abilities.

6. Interpersonal Psychotherapy (IPT): IPT is a brief form of therapy that aims to enhance communication and interpersonal interactions. It can be beneficial for those with AvPD who have trouble establishing and sustaining wholesome relationships.

7. Psychodynamic Therapy: In psychodynamic therapy, underlying conflicts and patterns that may be responsible for AvPD symptoms are investigated. Increasing self-awareness and comprehension of how prior experiences affect present behavior are its goals.

8. While counseling is the main course of treatment for AvPD, medication may occasionally be administered to alleviate the anxiety or depressive symptoms that frequently accompany AvPD. Medication needs to be

taken in conjunction with therapy and under a mental health professional's supervision.

Depending on the particular needs and preferences of the patient, different therapeutic modalities may be chosen. To choose the best course of treatment, people with AvPD should consult frequently with a licensed mental health specialist. The most efficient strategy to treat avoidant personality disorder and enhance general well-being is frequently through the use of a combination of therapeutic techniques that are customized to the person's particular issues.

The Function of Medicine

When co-occurring illnesses like anxiety or depression also exist in an individual with avoidant personality disorder (AvPD), medication may help treat the disease. Even though medicine is not a primary or stand-alone treatment for AvPD, it can be incorporated within a thorough treatment plan to target particular symptoms and enhance general well-being. Here are some advantages of medication:

1. Managing Anxiety: Significant anxiety is a common symptom of AvPD, particularly in social circumstances. To treat anxiety symptoms, doctors may prescribe drugs like benzodiazepines or selective serotonin reuptake inhibitors (SSRIs). Because they can treat both anxiety and depression, SSRIs are often utilized.

2. Managing Depression: People with AVPD frequently experience co-occurring depression. Antidepressant drugs, such as SSRIs or other varieties, can help treat depressed symptoms and elevate mood.

3. Mood stabilization: Some people with AvPD may experience mood changes or strong emotional responses that are connected to their avoidance strategies. When mood swings are a serious concern, mood stabilizers, such as lithium or specific anticonvulsants, may be taken into consideration.

4. Enhancing Treatment Response: By lessening the severity of anxiety or depression, medication can support psychotherapy. This makes it simpler for people to attend therapy sessions and concentrate on modifying avoidance habits and cognitive patterns.

It's important to remember that a licensed psychiatrist or healthcare provider normally prescribes and oversees AvPD medication. The precise symptoms of the person, their general health, and any potential drug interactions will all be taken into consideration when determining the prescription and dose.

Because it doesn't address the ingrained cognitive patterns and behavioral patterns connected to the condition, medication alone cannot treat AvPD. As a result, psychotherapy—especially cognitive-behavioral therapy (CBT), which is the main therapeutic strategy for AvPD—is frequently used with it.

In the context of treating AvPD, medication is used to manage symptoms, lessen emotional discomfort, improve a patient's capacity to participate fully in therapy and concentrate on improving their social skills and coping mechanisms. When necessary, the combination of therapy and medication can provide a thorough and all-encompassing strategy for controlling AvPD and enhancing general quality of life.

Choosing the Best Treatment Group

To receive helpful and successful therapy, people with Avoidant Personality Disorder (AvPD) must find the correct treatment team. To find the best treatment team, follow these steps:

1. Make an appointment with your primary care physician (PCP) to start: Make an appointment with your primary care physician (PCP) to start. Talk about your AvPD symptoms and worries. Your primary care physician (PCP) can refer you to mental health professionals and suggest the best tests.

2. Find a Qualified Mental Health Professional: Look for mental health specialists who focus on treating anxiety disorders, personality problems, or similar illnesses. Psychiatrists, psychologists, and clinical social workers with a license may fall under this category.

3. Ask for Recommendations: Request referrals from reliable people, such as friends, family members, or medical professionals. They might be able to recommend mental health specialists with AvPD experience.

4. Verify Credentials: Check the qualifications and credentials of the mental health specialists you are contemplating. Make sure they are qualified and have expertise in treating AvPD or disorders that are similar.

5. Consider scheduling first meetings or interviews with mental health specialists to go about your concerns and treatment objectives. This can assist you in determining

whether you are at ease and confident with the therapist's method.

6. Ask about the therapeutic methods that the mental health specialists employ when discussing treatment techniques. The therapist must be knowledgeable in cognitive-behavioral therapy (CBT), as it's frequently advised for AvPD. Other therapeutic approaches, however, might also be useful.

7. Look for therapists or mental health facilities that provide group therapy sessions exclusively for people with AVPD or social anxiety if you're interested in this option.

8. Consider Location and Accessibility When evaluating accessibility, take into account the office's location and accessibility. Your capacity to participate in regular therapy sessions can be significantly impacted by accessibility.

9. Review Insurance Coverage: If you have health insurance, find out which mental health professionals are covered by your plan by contacting your provider. You can control treatment costs by doing this.

10. Trust Your Gut: In the end, when selecting a treatment team, trust your gut. Your therapeutic alliance and level of comfort with your mental health professional are essential for a positive therapy experience.

11. Collaborative Care: To address many elements of their life and well-being, some people with AvPD may benefit from a multidisciplinary treatment team that includes a psychiatrist, therapist, and maybe other specialists (such as an occupational therapist or a vocational counselor).

Keep in mind that while locating the ideal treatment team may need some time and work, it will be worthwhile for your mental health and overall well-being. You may control AvPD and enhance your quality of life with the assistance of an effective treatment plan and the knowledge and support of your treatment team.

CHAPTER 5

Creating Coping Mechanisms

Behavioral-Cognitive Techniques

The mainstay of the avoidant personality disorder (AvPD) treatment is cognitive-behavioral therapy (CBT). CBT seeks to assist people with AVPD in recognizing and altering harmful thought patterns and actions that fuel their avoidance and social anxiety. The following cognitive-behavioral methods are frequently employed to treat AvPD:

1. Finding Negative Thought Patterns: People with AvPD frequently experience automatic negative thoughts about self-worth, social circumstances, and rejection anxiety. CBT enables patients to recognize these harmful thought patterns and pinpoint particular thoughts that cause anxiety and avoidance.

2. Challenge Cognitive Distortions: Cognitive behavioral therapy (CBT) helps people to question distorted or unreasonable thinking. This entails weighing the facts for and against their unfavorable assumptions and swapping them out with more pragmatic and impartial viewpoints.

3. Desensitization and Exposure: A vital part of CBT for AvPD is exposure therapy. In a controlled and methodical manner, people eventually approach fearful social circumstances or interactions. They become less sensitive to their worries as a result of this exposure, and their social skills improve.

4. The purpose of behavioral experiments is to test out novel behaviors and hypotheses in practical settings. This can assist people in gathering proof to refute their avoidance strategies and limiting beliefs.

5. Creating Coping Mechanisms: CBT teaches people particular coping mechanisms to control their anxiety in

social situations. This can involve mindfulness activities, deep breathing exercises, and relaxation techniques.

6. Social Skills Training: Many people with AVPD are socially ineffective. To help people get better at starting and keeping up conversations, expressing themselves clearly, and participating in social interactions more easily, CBT may incorporate social skills training.

7. Setting Achievable and Realistic Goals CBT assists people in setting realistic goals for social interaction. Starting with tiny, attainable steps and building up to more difficult situations can be a gradual process.

8. Role-playing activities in therapy give patients the chance to practice social skills and get feedback from their therapist. This can boost self-assurance and enhance communication abilities.

9. Self-monitoring: Keeping a journal or record of your avoidance and social anxiety-related thoughts, feelings,

and actions can help you gain important insights and monitor your progress during therapy.

10. Cognitive Restructuring: Cognitive restructuring is substituting more uplifting and helpful self-statements for negative self-talk. People learn to confront and swap out negative or scary beliefs with positive and realistic ones.

11. Exercises to be practiced outside of treatment sessions are frequently given as homework by therapists. These homework assignments support ongoing development by reinforcing the therapeutically acquired abilities.

With an emphasis on establishing specific treatment objectives and monitoring advancement, CBT for AvPD is often carried out in a controlled and time-limited style. To use these approaches effectively and to customize them to their own needs and challenges, people must work closely with a licensed therapist who has received

CBT training. CBT can eventually assist people with AvPD in establishing healthier thought and behavior patterns, lowering avoidance, and enhancing social interaction skills.

Desensitization and Exposition

Social anxiety and avoidant personality disorder (AvPD) are both treated with the therapy methods of exposure and desensitization. These cognitive-behavioral therapy (CBT) strategies are made to assist people in gradually confronting and overcoming their phobias associated with social situations. Let's examine exposure and desensitization in more detail:

Therapy for Exposure:

• Gradual Exposure: Exposure treatment includes systematically exposing patients to circumstances or stimuli that make them anxious or make them avoid behaviors. This exposure is carried out in a secure and controlled setting.

`

• Hierarchy of Fear: Individuals and therapists collaborate to establish a hierarchy of social circumstances or encounters that are feared. From least to most anxiety-provoking, circumstances are ranked in this hierarchy.

• Step-by-Step Approach: The person practices and approaches each issue on the hierarchy one at a time, beginning with the least anxiety-inducing one. This could start with visualizing the circumstance, move on to role-playing, and finally involve taking part in a real-life scenario.

• Repetition: It's crucial to repeat exposure activities. Individuals who are repeatedly exposed to their worry become accustomed to it and learn that their feared outcomes (such as rejection or embarrassment) are less likely to occur than they think.

• Coping tactics: During exposure, people pick up and put into practice coping tactics including deep breathing, cognitive restructuring, and relaxation methods to help them control their anxiety.

• Positive Reinforcement: Positive comments and acknowledgment of progress are used to promote effective exposure activities. This may give you more confidence and drive to keep on with your exposure.

Desensitization:

• Emotional desensitization: Desensitization is the process of being less sensitive or emotionally reactive to situations or stimuli that cause worry. It entails lowering the terror response's emotional ferocity.

• Repeated Exposure: Desensitization helps people develop a tolerance for their anxiety and lessens the emotional impact of these circumstances over time by regularly exposing them to feared social settings in a gradual and controlled way.

• Shift in Emotional Reaction: Through desensitization, people may experience a change in their emotional reaction from extreme dread and anxiety to a more controllable degree of discomfort or even indifference.

• Improved Coping: As people grow less sensitive to the things that make them feel anxious in social situations, they frequently find it easier to use the coping skills they've developed in treatment, like cognitive restructuring and relaxation methods.

Because exposure and desensitization specifically address avoidance tendencies and social anxiety, they are effective treatments for people with AVPD. Individuals can gradually broaden their comfort zones, enhance their social involvement, and gain more self-assurance in handling social situations with the help of a qualified therapist. These methods are a component of a thorough therapy strategy that also entails other cognitive-behavioral tactics to combat unfavorable thought patterns and encourage healthy social connections.

Relaxation and Stress Reduction

For people with avoidant personality disorder (AvPD), stress management and relaxation strategies can be helpful tools for managing anxiety and enhancing general well-being. These methods can support exposure therapy and cognitive-behavioral therapy (CBT) in helping people manage their stress and anxiety in social situations. Here are some methods for calming down and relieving tension that can be useful:

1. Deep breathing exercises entail taking long, slow breaths to reduce tension in the body. It can ease tension and reduce feelings of anxiety. Try breathing in for four counts, holding for seven, and then exhaling for eight counts using the 4-7-8 breathing technique.

2. Progressive Muscle Relaxation: Using this technique, various body parts' muscle groups are sequentially tense and then relaxed. It encourages relaxation and aids in the release of physical stress.

3. Being fully present in the present moment and accepting one's thoughts and feelings without passing judgment are the main goals of mindfulness meditation. Regular mindfulness training can help you become more self-aware and less anxious.

4. Yoga: Yoga blends physical postures with breathing techniques, meditation, and stress reduction. Additionally, it can aid in increasing physical health and flexibility.

5. Guided imaging: With guided imagery, you can picture serene scenes in your head. It might be a good method to calm down and get away from upsetting thoughts.

6. Autogenic Training: To achieve a relaxed state through autogenic training, a sequence of self-suggestions is repeated. Some of these sentences can be "I am calm" or "My body is relaxed."

7. Aromatherapy: Some fragrances, like lavender or chamomile, are well-known for their calming and

unwinding properties. Candles, diffusers, or essential oils can all be utilized in aromatherapy treatments.

8. Journaling: Keeping a journal can help you manage emotions and lessen stress by allowing you to write down your ideas and feelings. It can also be a helpful tool for monitoring therapy progress.

9. Exercise: Regular physical activity, such as jogging, swimming, or walking, helps lower stress and elevate mood. Endorphins, which are endorphin-based stress relievers, are released when you exercise.

10. Social Support: Spending time with encouraging friends and family members might help you feel less lonely and relieve your emotions. Being able to express your worries and experiences to reliable people can be helpful.

11. Time management: Useful time management strategies can lessen stress caused by job or daily

`

obligations. Setting objectives and organizing work might make people feel more in charge of their lives.

12. Guided relaxation exercises, mindfulness meditations, and stress-reduction methods are all available through a wide variety of relaxation apps and online resources. These are simple to use and can be accessed when necessary.

People with AvPD must experiment with and put numerous relaxation techniques to the test to find the ones that suit them the most. These approaches can help people feel less anxious, be more emotionally resilient, and be better able to handle social settings. Additionally, incorporating relaxing methods into regular activities can improve general well-being and boost the efficacy of AvPD therapy.

CHAPTER 6

Creating Stable Relationships

Having conversations with loved ones

Even though communicating with loved ones can be difficult when you have Avoidant Personality Disorder (AvPD), it's crucial for creating and preserving positive connections. Following are some pointers for having fruitful conversations with loved ones while managing AvPD:

1. Self-awareness: Start by becoming aware of how your AvPD impacts your emotions, thoughts, and actions in social settings. Effective communication begins with awareness of your difficulties.

2. Educate Your Loved Ones: Inform your family members about AvPD. Help them comprehend the disorder's characteristics, as well as your social anxiety

`

and fear of rejection. Empathy and support can be fostered via education.

3. Open and Honest Communication: Try to be open and honest with those you care about. Openly express your views, feelings, and worries, even if it makes you uncomfortable. Speaking openly about your difficulties might increase support and understanding.

4. Set Reasonable Expectations: Ensure that your loved ones have reasonable expectations about your capacity to interact socially. Clarify the types of social engagements you are comfortable with and mention that you might require breaks or time alone.

5. Use "I" phrases: When expressing your wants or feelings, use "I" phrases to avoid placing blame or making accusations. Instead of saying "You make me anxious in large gatherings," try saying "I feel anxious in large social gatherings."

6. Request Feedback: Request constructive criticism from your loved ones about your social interactions. Request their feedback on how you may enhance your efforts to help them feel more at ease.

7. When your loved ones share their views and worries with you, engage in active listening. Giving them your entire attention and acknowledging their feelings will demonstrate empathy and understanding.

8. Ask for Patience: Inform your loved ones that it can take some time for you to make progress in managing AvPD. As you practice being social and confront your concerns, ask for their understanding and assistance.

9. Set Boundaries: Make it clear to others what you expect in terms of social interactions and personal space. When you're feeling overwhelmed, it's acceptable to assertively state that you need some alone time or space.

10. Celebrate Small Wins: Tell your loved ones about your accomplishments and little wins in social situations. Together, we can celebrate these victories, which can create a good and encouraging environment.

11. Include Them in Your Treatment: Include your loved ones in the AvPD treatment or therapy you are undergoing. They can find out what your therapy objectives are and how they can help.

12. Seek Couples or Family Therapy: If your AvPD is significantly straining your relationships, think about seeking couples or family therapy. A therapist can assist all parties in understanding and meeting each other's needs while facilitating communication.

Always keep in mind that good communication is a talent that can be developed through time. It's acceptable to make errors and to ask for help when necessary. Even though managing AvPD requires effort, you may create and maintain healthy relationships with your loved ones with a little knowledge and practice.

Closeness and Social Interactions

Due to their anxiety and fear of rejection, people with Avoidant Personality Disorder (AvPD) may find intimacy and social bonds difficult. However, with some techniques and assistance, it is possible to forge genuine connections and enjoy closeness, both in friendships and love partnerships:

1. Accepting yourself and your AvPD is the first step. Recognize that even if you face special difficulties, you are deserving of love and connection. Building connections requires a strong foundation of self-acceptance.

2. Seek Therapy: Attend therapy sessions, especially cognitive-behavioral therapy (CBT), to address the underlying assumptions and avoidance patterns

connected to AvPD. You can confront unhelpful thought habits and improve your social abilities through therapy.

3. Gradual Exposure: With the help of a therapist, expose yourself gradually to social circumstances that make you anxious. This can help you become less sensitive to those circumstances over time and increase your confidence in handling them.

4. Join Support Groups: Take into account joining social clubs or support groups based on your interests or hobbies. These might offer a more laid-back and organized approach to meeting individuals who share your interests.

5. Develop Social Skills: Put your attention into practicing and developing social skills through treatment. Effective communication, active listening, and empathy for others can all be examples of this.

6. Set Achievable Goals: Establish realistic objectives for social interactions. Begin with easy measures, such as

briefly attending a social function, and raise your level of involvement over time.

7. Make self-care a priority if you want to manage your stress and anxiety. Better mental health and social connections can be facilitated by getting enough sleep, exercising, and eating a balanced diet.

8. Challenge Negative Beliefs: Constantly refute unfavorable assumptions about both yourself and other people. Keep in mind that not all conversations will result in rejection because not everyone is critical or judgmental.

9. Be nice and sympathetic to oneself by practicing self-compassion. You should approach yourself with the same compassion and understanding as you would a friend.

10. Learn how to communicate effectively, including how to honestly and forcefully express your opinions

and feelings. For partnerships to grow in closeness and trust, effective communication is crucial.

11. Open Up Gradually: As you establish trust in new connections, it's acceptable to open up gradually. Slowly express your views and feelings while allowing the connection to grow at its own pace.

12. Seek Professional Advice for Romantic Connections: If you want to pursue romantic connections, you might want to think about getting advice from a therapist or counselor who specializes in relationship issues. They can offer guidance and coping mechanisms for dealing with closeness and attachment.

13. Maintain Existing Relationships: Don't forget to maintain your current friendships and connections. Keeping in touch with encouraging friends and family members can provide one with a feeling of safety and belonging.

Keep in mind that developing closeness and social ties takes time and that obstacles are a normal part of the road. When experiencing difficulties, seek help from friends, family, or a therapist, and remember to recognize your accomplishments along the road. People with AvPD can establish meaningful and fulfilling social ties with the right amount of time and effort.

Setting Limits and Practicing Self-Care

For people with Avoidant Personality Disorder (AvPD), setting boundaries and engaging in self-care is essential to managing their well-being, lowering anxiety, and preserving healthy relationships. The following are some techniques for establishing boundaries and engaging in self-care:

Establishing Boundaries

1. Your emotional and physical needs in diverse circumstances and relationships should be identified.

Setting limits begins with being aware of your requirements.

2. Clarify Your Communication: Be forceful in your communication to clearly and politely state your boundaries. To express your demands and feelings without blaming or accusing others, use "I" statements.

3. Start Small: Start by establishing limits in low-risk circumstances. For instance, if you require some alone time to recharge, respectfully let a friend or loved one know when necessary.

4. Set Self-Care as a Priority: Organize your time so that you can give yourself the attention you need. This can entail setting aside regular time for self-care activities like solitude or relaxation techniques.

5. Learn to Say "No": Get in the habit of rejecting invitations and requests by simply saying "no." You don't have to accept everything, and it's acceptable to put your health first.

6. Set Repercussions: Establish repercussions for crossing your boundaries. For instance, decide what action you will take to maintain your boundaries if someone continually enters your personal space or disregards your need for alone time.

7. Seek Support: Discuss your intentions for setting boundaries with a counselor, support group, or close friend. They can offer advice and motivation as you practice this skill.

Self-Care Exercise:

1. Know Your Triggers: Recognize the circumstances or experiences that make you anxious or prone to avoidance. Knowing your triggers will make it easier for you to control them.

2. Establish a regular self-care schedule that includes activities that encourage relaxation and lower stress. This could involve hobbies you enjoy, exercise, journaling, or meditation.

3. Be honest with yourself about what you can do in a day or a week when setting your goals. Refrain from taking on too much and causing yourself stress.

4. Healthy Lifestyle: Make physical health a top priority by eating a balanced diet, exercising frequently, and getting enough sleep. Mental health can be strongly impacted by physical well-being.

5. Practice mindfulness and meditation practices to stay centered in the here and now and lessen worry about upcoming social engagements.

6. Reduce Stressor Exposure: Avoid being around people or situations that frequently make your AvPD symptoms worse. For yourself, create a secure and encouraging environment.

7. Be nice and sympathetic to oneself by practicing self-compassion. Recognize that despite your difficulties, you deserve respect, love, and self-care.

8. Seek expert Assistance: If self-care seems difficult or ineffective, think about getting advice from a mental health expert who can develop self-care techniques that are tailored to your individual needs.

9. Make Time for Enjoyable Activities: Schedule time for pursuits that make you feel happy and fulfilled. These pursuits can operate as healthy decompression mechanisms for tension and stress.

10. Support network: Stay in touch with friends or family members who can understand your struggles and provide emotional support when required.

Keep in mind that establishing boundaries and caring for yourself are continual tasks. As you discover what works best for you, it's acceptable to make modifications. Setting your health as a top priority will help you manage AvPD and enhance your general quality of life.

Chapter 7

Success Stories and Insights from Thriving Beyond Avoidance

Real-World Success Tales

It's crucial to understand that people with avoidant personality disorder (AvPD) can make substantial progress in controlling their symptoms and succeeding in numerous facets of life, even though it can create significant problems. Here are a few examples of people who have successfully overcome AvPD in real life:

1. John's Path to a Meaningful Career John battled AvPD throughout his adolescence and avoided social situations and employment possibilities. He eventually gained confidence after going to counseling and using exposure tactics. He now has rewarding employment as a teacher, interacting regularly with both pupils and coworkers.

2. Anna's Success in Social Relationships: Anna struggled to establish and sustain relationships because of her acute social anxiety brought on by AvPD. She gained the ability to confront her unfavorable ideas and participate in social activities through regular counseling and support groups. She now has a loving partner and a close-knit group of pals.

3. David's Public Speaking Development: Due to David's AvPD, speaking in front of an audience was extremely difficult. His public speaking abilities gradually improved with the aid of therapy and practice. He then achieved popularity as a motivational speaker, sharing his story and motivating others through AvPD.

4. Sarah's Path to Higher Education: Because of her AvPD-related worries about academic and interpersonal failure, Sarah initially decided against going to college. She went to counseling to deal with her avoidance tendencies and self-esteem problems, and as a result, she was able to finish college and now works as a

counselor, assisting others in overcoming similar difficulties.

5. Mike's Success in Creating Support Networks: Due to his AvPD, Mike felt alone for a long time before deciding to get help. He steadily widened his social network with the aid of counseling and self-help literature. He now takes part in social clubs, gives back to the community, and has a network of friends who are encouraging.

6. Emily's Path to Personal Growth: Both in her personal and professional life, Emily's AvPD held her back. She set out on a voyage of self-discovery and progress with tenacity and expert guidance. Since then, she has followed a rewarding job and delights in meaningful connections.

These success stories demonstrate that people with AvPD can make great progress in managing their symptoms, enhancing their self-esteem, and creating happy lives with the correct help, therapy, and personal commitment. These cases show that it is possible to go above AvPD's restrictions and have a fulfilling life, even though the road to success may be difficult.

Techniques for a Prolonged Recover

Long-term rehabilitation from Avoidant Personality Disorder (AvPD) entails consistent work and dedication to symptom management, fostering positive interpersonal connections, and enhancing general well-being. The following are techniques for sustained recovery:

1. Consistent Therapy: Keep going to therapy even when you see some early progress. Your success can be maintained and any relapses or new problems can be addressed with long-term therapy, which includes maintenance sessions.

2. Medication Management: If you're taking medication to treat anxiety or depressive symptoms, get in touch

with the doctor who prescribed it so they can check on your progress and make necessary adjustments.

3. Develop Self-Awareness: Be conscious of your AvPD-related thoughts, feelings, and behaviors. Utilizing coping mechanisms and early detection of undesirable tendencies are made possible by self-awareness.

4. Self-Help tools: As an adjunct to therapy, use self-help books, workbooks, and online tools. These resources can provide you with more resources and recovery-supporting workouts.

5. Social Support: Keep a solid network of friends and family that can relate to your struggles and offer emotional support. Maintain contact and let them know how things are going.

6. Set Achievable Goals: Consistently set goals that are doable for you in terms of your social interactions and personal development. Celebrate your accomplishments and thank yourself for your efforts.

7. Increase Resilience: Increase your ability to bounce back from setbacks and challenging circumstances. This calls for overcoming obstacles, coping with stress, and overcoming setbacks.

Keep broadening your comfort zones by gradually exposing yourself to novel social circumstances and difficulties. Over time, more exposure makes you more at ease.

9. Develop Self-Compassion: Be patient and gentle to yourself. Recognize that setbacks are a normal part of the healing process, and that self-compassion can help you recover and carry on moving forward.

10. Lifestyle Decisions: Maintain a focus on leading a healthy lifestyle, which includes frequent exercise, a balanced diet, enough sleep, and stress reduction. Mental health and physical well-being are tightly related.

11. Maintaining mindfulness and relaxation methods will help you manage stress and anxiety. You may maintain your composure and presence in social situations by using these tactics.

12. Schedule Regular Check-Ins: Even if you're feeling fine, schedule regular check-ins with your therapist. These sessions can aid with relapse prevention and can address any new difficulties.

13. Community Involvement: Take part in volunteer work or community events. This can offer possibilities for social connection and a sense of purpose while also giving back to others.

14. Monitor Negative Thought Patterns: Use cognitive-behavioral approaches to confront and reframe negative thought patterns associated with AvPD.

15. Continue Your Education: Keep up your knowledge of AvPD, therapeutic approaches, and improvements in

mental health care. Being informed gives you the power to actively participate in your rehabilitation.

AvPD healing is a process, and there will likely be ups and downs along the route. Seek assistance and continue to work on your long-term recovery objectives. Living a happy life with AvPD is feasible with effort and the appropriate approaches.